Original title:
Creative Instincts

Author: Hanna Helimets
ISBN HARDBACK: 978-9916-87-720-3
ISBN PAPERBACK: 978-9916-87-721-0
ISBN EBOOK: 978-9916-87-722-7

Dreams Stitched with Light

In the quiet of the night,
Whispers weave through stars bright.
Threads of silver softly blend,
Creating dreams that never end.

Moonlight drapes on silver seams,
Painting worlds born of our dreams.
Flickering hopes in every hue,
Stitched with light, forever true.

Through shadows where the heart may dwell,
Secrets unravel, stories to tell.
In the fabric, we find our place,
A tapestry of time and space.

Every stitch, a moment caught,
Woven memories, lessons taught.
From the past, a future gleams,
Hope restored in stitched-up dreams.

So close your eyes and drift away,
Into the night where dreamers stay.
In this realm, our spirits take flight,
Together weave dreams stitched with light.

Inspiration's Dance

In the stillness, ideas bloom,
Lightly drifting, dispelling gloom.
A spark ignites, a fire pure,
Moving hearts, creating allure.

Footsteps follow a beat so sweet,
Inspiration sways, a rhythmic feat.
With every turn, new paths appear,
Bringing visions ever near.

Colors swirl in joyous play,
Thoughts embrace the light of day.
In the dance of minds so free,
Artistry flows, a melody.

With fervent grace, we intertwine,
Dreams become a vibrant line.
In the echoes of our trance,
Life unfolds in inspiration's dance.

So take my hand, let's weave anew,
Let passion guide in all we do.
Together in this sacred trance,
We celebrate inspiration's dance.

The Alchemy of Thought

In the cauldron, ideas churn,
Transforming till the heart can learn.
Gold emerges from leaden dreams,
The alchemy of thought redeems.

With every glance, perception shifts,
Turning doubts into precious gifts.
A whisper sparks the fire of think,
Inviting minds to dive and sink.

Let shadows play, let daylight seep,
In silence where the secrets keep.
Breathing deep the unseen soul,
Crafting life with purpose whole.

In every thought, a world concealed,
With vision clear, our fate revealed.
Alchemy flows through heart and mind,
Transforming life, our essence refined.

So ponder well, in quiet space,
Unlock the door, embrace the grace.
With every moment, weave and wrought,
We find the magic in thought.

Unleashed Brushstrokes

With every stroke, a story spins,
Canvas breathes where the heart begins.
Colors dance in vibrant hues,
Whispers of what the artist views.

Freedom flows in each bold line,
As thoughts collide, create, align.
The brushes glide, chaos becomes,
A masterpiece that softly hums.

In flashes bright, emotions surge,
Within the art, our spirits merge.
Unleashed from bounds that once confined,
A world anew, a gift defined.

Layer by layer, dreams take flight,
Chasing shadows, pulling light.
Art reveals what words can't say,
Unleashed brushstrokes lead the way.

So take the plunge, express your soul,
Let creativity make you whole.
In every mark, our hearts invoke,
Life's beauty born from unleashed stroke.

Symphony of Ideas

In the quiet night we dream,
Thoughts like rivers softly stream.
Notes of wisdom fill the air,
Harmony in minds laid bare.

Voices rise in gentle rhyme,
Dancing through the threads of time.
Each idea a vibrant hue,
A canvas wide, an endless view.

Melodies of peace unfold,
In every story, truth is told.
A symphony that lifts the soul,
Uniting pieces to make whole.

From whispers born in silence deep,
To echoes where the muses leap.
Each spark ignites a path ahead,
While echoes play of words unsaid.

Together we compose a song,
In this realm where we belong.
A symphony of hearts and minds,
In every note, new hope we find.

The Heart's Palette

Brushes dipped in love's embrace,
Colors swirling, time and space.
A canvas waits for strokes divine,
Each hue a heartbeat, pure design.

Reds ignite the fires within,
Blues bring calm, let dreams begin.
Greens of growth, like springtime's bloom,
Shades of dusk invite us to swoon.

With every layer, stories rise,
Whispers painted in the skies.
The heart's creations come alive,
In vibrant notes, our spirits thrive.

Pastel memories blend and fade,
While bold intentions refuse to shade.
Each stroke a tale, each line a chance,
To dance anew in love's expanse.

In this palette we create,
A masterpiece that won't abate.
With open hearts, we blend our art,
Creating beauty from the start.

Whims of the Daring

Beneath the stars, we chase the bold,
Stories waiting to be told.
Feet unbound, we take the leap,
Into the wild, our dreams we keep.

The winds of change, they call our name,
With every step, we lose the tame.
Daring hearts, we fly and spin,
Embracing life, we lose and win.

Joy and chaos intertwine,
Navigating fate's design.
Through laughter, tears, and moments rare,
In glorious leaps, we find our air.

With fearless souls, we carve our path,
Creating joy, igniting wrath.
Whims of daring, wild and free,
Together we shape our destiny.

In twilight's glow, our spirits rise,
Chasing dreams beneath the skies.
With every heartbeat, strong and true,
The daring dance, just me and you.

Echoes of Inspiration

Whispers in the morning light,
Gentle sparks that ignite the night.
A breeze that carries dreams so high,
In every heart, a reason why.

With every thought, a world can blend,
Our voices lift, they never end.
Ideas flow like rivers wide,
Inspiration’s journey, our guide.

Through shadows cast, a spark appears,
In every challenge, conquer fears.
Moments shared, our stories blend,
A tapestry that has no end.

Voices rise, a symphony,
In echoes, we find unity.
From hopes and dreams, we paint our view,
Inspiration's light, a vibrant hue.

Together we explore the vast,
Creating futures, freeing pasts.
With echoes strong, we face the day,
Inspiration leads us on our way.

Brushstrokes of the Mind

In colors bright and shadows deep,
Thoughts collide, dreams softly seep.
A canvas stretched, awaiting flair,
Emotions dance in vibrant air.

Each stroke unveils a hidden tale,
Whispers echo, soft and frail.
Imagination's vivid sea,
Brushstrokes shaped by what could be.

A palette rich, with hopes imbued,
Each hue reflects a heart renewed.
From chaos comes tranquility,
In painted realms, we wander free.

With every layer, wisdom grows,
Silent truths in color flows.
The mind, a painter, rich and bold,
In hues of life, our stories told.

So let us journey, brush in hand,
Creating visions, oh so grand.
For in this art, we find our way,
In brushstrokes bright, we learn to play.

Illuminated Journeys

Beneath the stars, we set our sails,
In twilight's glow, adventure prevails.
Paths uncharted call our names,
Each step a dance, igniting flames.

The lanterns flicker, guiding light,
Through shadowed woods and endless night.
With every heartbeat, fear must fade,
In journeys bold, our dreams are made.

Together we climb, against the tide,
In whispered winds, our hopes abide.
Through valleys vast and mountains steep,
Illuminated, our souls leap.

With every sunrise, fresh and bright,
We chase the dawn, embracing flight.
For every moment holds a spark,
A journey’s joy, igniting the dark.

So let the path be free, unbound,
In every turn, new treasures found.
With hearts ablaze, we forge ahead,
Illuminated journeys, bright and red.

Threads of Vision

Woven dreams, like silken strands,
Intertwined by unseen hands.
A tapestry of hope we weave,
In every thread, we dare believe.

The patterns dance, unique and grand,
With colors bold, we take our stand.
Through trials faced and victories won,
Threads of vision spun as one.

Glimmers shine in darkest night,
Guiding hearts towards the light.
In every fiber, stories lie,
Each woven thread a whispered sigh.

The loom of fate, a gentle sway,
We craft our lives in bright array.
With every knot, a moment seized,
Threads of vision, hearts appeased.

So let us stitch with love and care,
In every thread, a dream to share.
For in this fabric, we will find,
The strength that flows through threads of mind.

The Symphony of Potential

In silence waits a perfect note,
A melody in dreams remote.
Each moment holds a vibrant sound,
A symphony of life unbound.

With hearts attuned to rhythms true,
We dance to tunes both old and new.
An orchestra of hopes arise,
In every chord, the spirit flies.

As crescendos build, aspirations swell,
The story of our lives to tell.
With harmony, we’ll brave the storm,
In every clash, new forms are born.

In whispered tones, the secrets flow,
Each pause a chance for love to grow.
Together, let our voices blend,
In symphonic grace, the soul can mend.

So play the song that stirs your heart,
In every beat, we take our part.
For in this symphony, we thrive,
Potential's tune, alive, alive.

Symphony of Shadows

In twilight's gentle embrace,
Whispers float through the air,
A dance of dark and light,
Filled with moments to share.

Each note a secret told,
Echoes in the still night,
Melodies unfold,
Beneath the silver light.

Ghosts of memories roam,
In corners where we tread,
Their stories call us home,
In the silence, they're fed.

Through branches, shadows weave,
Nature's breath softly sighs,
In the heart, we believe,
As starlight gently lies.

The night, a symphony,
Each heartbeat turns the page,
In the stillness, we see,
The dance of every age.

Echoes of the Unknown

In the depths of the night,
Strange whispers take their flight,
Questions fill the dark sky,
With secrets begging why.

Footsteps on roads untraveled,
Adventures yet to start,
Through fog, once unraveled,
We seek with an open heart.

In shadows, stories sleep,
Awaiting to be found,
In silence, secrets creep,
In echoes, they resound.

Stars above twinkle bright,
Guiding the curious soul,
Through the lingering night,
Towards the vast unknown goal.

Every dream yet to chase,
Calls us to explore,
To embrace every place,
And unlock each hidden door.

Tides of Discovery

Waves crashing on the shore,
Secrets of ages past,
Pulling us to explore,
Where time flows unsurpassed.

With each tide, lessons learn,
Nature's rhythm in sway,
In the stillness, we yearn,
For the dawn of a new day.

Shores whisper tales anew,
In sand, they etch their mark,
A canvas wide and blue,
Where dreams ignite a spark.

With shells to guide our way,
We wander side by side,
In the light of the day,
While the ocean turns the tide.

Every ebb, every flow,
Reveals a hidden truth,
In the depths, we will grow,
Uncovering our lost youth.

Palette of the Heart

Brush strokes of vibrant hues,
Every color speaks loud,
In silence, dreams infused,
Where the heart feels so proud.

Canvas of life laid bare,
With each moment defined,
Impressions made with care,
By the spirit entwined.

A splash of love, a tear,
A blend of joy and pain,
In this art we hold dear,
A masterpiece from the plain.

Through shades of deep despair,
To brilliance in the light,
Every layer a prayer,
Painting shadows to bright.

As brushes dance and twirl,
In rhythm with the beat,
Life's canvas starts to swirl,
Creating a world complete.

A Canvas of Epiphanies

Colors swirl in vivid light,
Dreams awaken, taking flight.
Brushstrokes dance, whispers call,
A canvas holds the truth of all.

Moments captured, fleeting time,
In each layer, stories climb.
Imagined worlds paint my soul,
With every hue, I feel more whole.

Bright splashes bring a tear of joy,
With every stroke, I must enjoy.
Transforming pain into delight,
The canvas shines, dispelling night.

A palette rich, emotions flow,
In silence deep, the colors grow.
An artist's heart, it learns to see,
The beauty found in reverie.

With every brush, my spirit sings,
A journey through what meaning brings.
A tapestry, both bold and bright,
Epiphanies of purest light.

Unraveling the Silence

In the stillness, whispers blend,
Echoes of the heart, they tend.
Words unspoken float in air,
Secrets linger everywhere.

The quiet speaks in gentle tones,
Each pause resounds, like silent drones.
Listen close, for what's concealed,
In silence, truths are revealed.

Fading echoes of yesterday,
In the void, my thoughts array.
Between each breath, a mystic song,
In solitude, where I belong.

Voices dance in shadowed light,
Unraveling thoughts, taking flight.
Each nuance holds a tale profound,
In the silence, wisdom's found.

With every beat, the heart relates,
To the stillness that resonates.
Unraveling the quiet strife,
Brings forth the beauty of our life.

Notes on a Blank Page

A vacant sheet, a world to write,
Dreams and thoughts in pure daylight.
With every mark, a story starts,
A canvas waits for open hearts.

Lines weave tales both bold and shy,
Words that dance and thoughts that fly.
Ink flows freely, hope contained,
In this space, I am unchained.

Each letter crafted, a piece of soul,
In brackets small, I find my whole.
Ideas bloom like flowers bright,
Painting visions, pure delight.

With strokes of thought upon the page,
I channel life's untamed rage.
From whispers soft to thunder's call,
In every line, I give my all.

In solitude, I carve my way,
Notes that linger, never fray.
A blank page waits, my heart's own stage,
In written lines, I am the sage.

Journey Through the Abstract

In realms where logic fades away,
I wander through the hues of gray.
A journey starts within my mind,
Where reason bends and truths unwind.

Shapes collide in playful dance,
Inviting me to take a chance.
Lost in thoughts, my spirit soars,
Through twisted paths, it freely roars.

The abstract beckons, wild and free,
A realm of pure creativity.
Each moment shifts, a fluid dream,
Where passion flows like a rushing stream.

I tread on lines of fate and choice,
In shadows deep, I find my voice.
Each thought a color, bold and bright,
Illuminating the quiet night.

With every twist, the journey calls,
A tapestry that never stalls.
Through abstract realms, I find my ground,
In every stroke, my truth is found.

The Alchemist of Dreams

In twilight's glow, he stirs the night,
With whispered spells of pure delight.
He turns the mundane into the gleam,
Crafting wonders from a silent dream.

A flicker here, a shimmer there,
Transforming shadows into air.
Through silver hands, the visions glide,
In alchemy, there's nothing to hide.

Each thought a thread, each sigh a key,
Unlocking realms for him to see.
With golden dust and magic's kiss,
He weaves a world of endless bliss.

The stars above, they start to dance,
In his embrace, they find a chance.
To travel paths yet to be made,
In every heart, his dreams cascade.

So close your eyes and take the flight,
Embrace the whispers of the night.
For in this space, where shadows teem,
You'll find the alchemist of dreams.

Whispering Shadows

In the stillness, shadows speak,
Softly weaving tales unique.
From corners dark, their secrets flow,
In whispers low, they come and go.

They flicker round with ghostly charms,
Caressing hearts, with silent arms.
Guiding souls through veils of night,
In their embrace, there’s hidden light.

With every sigh, the echoes breathe,
Weaving stories, a gossamer wreath.
Through ancient woods, they gently sway,
In twilight’s hush, they find their way.

While dreams may dance on silver beams,
Shadows cradle our deepest dreams.
In their language, forgotten lore,
We hear the songs of those before.

So linger long, let shadows call,
In their embrace, we’re free to fall.
For every whisper holds a truth,
A shadowed bond that leads to youth.

The Mind's Odyssey

A journey starts with a single thought,
In labyrinths where dreams are caught.
Through peaks and valleys, the mind will roam,
Seeking solace, searching for home.

In every twist, a new refrain,
In whispered hopes and hidden pain.
Through streams of light, the visions flow,
In the mind's eye, they gently grow.

With every step, the echoes chime,
Marking moments, lost in time.
Through portals vast, we weave and drift,
In the odyssey, the soul will lift.

Each thought a spark, igniting the night,
Painting landscapes, bathed in light.
With courage bold, we rise and soar,
In the heart's vault, forevermore.

So sail the seas of your own design,
Chart every course, let the stars align.
For in this quest, you'll surely find,
The endless depth of the mind’s kind.

Fantasies Illustrated

On pages worn, the tales unfold,
Adventures grand, in colors bold.
With ink and dreams, the stories flow,
As brush meets canvas, visions glow.

In every stroke, a world appears,
Laughter echoes, chase away fears.
From fairytale lands to skies of blue,
Fantasies woven with threads so true.

Characters dance in vibrant hue,
With hearts ablaze, they seek the new.
Through trials faced and battles fought,
In every chapter, lessons taught.

With eyes aglow, we turn the page,
Embarking on this timeless stage.
For in these tales, we find our own,
Fantasies illustrated, seeds are sown.

So let imagination lead the way,
Explore the realms where dreamers play.
For in these stories, we'll delight,
In worlds unbound, we take our flight.

Wandering Thoughts

In the quiet of the night,
Thoughts drift like whispers,
Elusive as the stars,
Fleeting in their presence.

Questioning the past,
Sailing on memories,
Each moment a treasure,
Hidden deep within me.

A breeze stirs the silence,
Carrying old echoes,
Glimmers of laughter,
Stories untold and free.

In shadows they linger,
Wandering like lost souls,
Yearning for a dawn,
To anchor them once more.

With every breath I take,
I gather these fragments,
A tapestry of dreams,
Woven in the twilight.

The Garden of Whimsy

Amidst the blooms of color,
Lies a world of delight,
Where laughter dances freely,
And shadows play in light.

Each petal tells a secret,
In whispers sweet and soft,
Inviting hearts to wander,
And let their spirits loft.

The breeze carries wishes,
On wings of pastel hues,
While butterflies twirl gently,
In a joyous, lovely muse.

Glimmers of elusive dreams,
In every corner live,
A garden filled with wonder,
Where imagination thrives.

As twilight starts to settle,
The stars begin to glow,
In this haven of whimsy,
Magic continues to flow.

Chasing Elysium

In the chase of the horizon,
Where sky meets the sea,
I dream of a lost paradise,
Where I long to be free.

With every footstep forward,
I seek the warmth of grace,
A whisper in the silence,
A soft, familiar place.

Time seems to slow down,
In the heart of the quest,
Each moment a treasure,
A heartbeat at its best.

Through valleys of amber,
And hills lush and green,
I chase the light of Elysium,
Living the sweet dream.

Underneath the starlight,
I find solace and peace,
In the arms of the night,
Where all struggles cease.

The Inked Journey

With ink upon the paper,
Stories begin to flow,
A journey of expression,
Where hidden thoughts can grow.

Each stroke tells a tale,
Of passion, loss, and love,
Threads of life entwined,
A tapestry thereof.

The pen becomes my compass,
Guiding through the dark,
Illuminating shadows,
Igniting the inner spark.

A voyage through the heart,
Where echoes find their voice,
In every written line,
The soul learns to rejoice.

As pages turn like seasons,
My voyage never ends,
Inked with every heartbeat,
Where the spirit transcends.

Grooves of Authenticity

In the heart, the rhythm plays,
A melody of different days.
Each step a mark, each breath a song,
In the dance where we all belong.

Voices rise and fall like tide,
Truth unmasked, no need to hide.
In the light of purest grace,
We find our strength, we find our place.

Time flows gently, whispers wise,
Dreams awakened, endless skies.
Through cracks of doubt, we let it shine,
In grooves of self, our souls align.

Vulnerability is our might,
In shadows, we embrace the light.
With every word, we break the mold,
A story shared, a wish retold.

Together, we write our own tale,
In authenticity, we will prevail.
With open hearts, we claim the day,
In this dance, we find our way.

Shadows of the Unconscious

In the stillness, shadows creep,
Whispers of secrets, buried deep.
Lost in the maze of dreams and fears,
We wander through the silent years.

Echoes of the past draw near,
In the dark, the visions clear.
Fractured thoughts lead us astray,
In the night, we hide away.

But in the depths, a spark ignites,
Awakening our inner sights.
We dance with ghosts, embrace the dread,
As shadows guide the words unsaid.

From chaos blooms a fragile truth,
In fragments lies the voice of youth.
In shadows' grip, we find our might,
Bringing colors into the night.

Through the veil, we seek the whole,
In darkness, we uncover our soul.
Emerge from depths, alive and bright,
In the shadows, we find the light.

The Echo Chamber of Invention

In the chamber, ideas collide,
Bouncing echoes, side by side.
Innovation's spark ignites,
In the dance of thoughts, it lights.

Voices blend, a symphony,
Each note a thread in tapestry.
Crafted visions take their form,
In the creative storm, we warm.

Waves of genius crash and break,
In the silence, ripples make.
Fragments turn to vibrant hue,
In every sound, a tale rings true.

Through laughter, doubt, and fervent play,
New ideas find their way to stay.
In our dreams, we cast the thread,
Invention's bloom, a joy widespread.

So we gather, minds afire,
In the echo chamber, we aspire.
From chaos springs a vision grand,
Together, we shape a world unplanned.

Dances in the Abyss

In the void where silence reigns,
We find the beauty in the pains.
Through shadows deep, we take our chance,
With whispered thoughts, we start to dance.

In darkness, mysteries unfold,
As secrets shyly do their gold.
With every step, we face the fear,
In the abyss, our truths appear.

The ground below seems far away,
Yet in the void, we long to stay.
With courage bold, we spin and twirl,
In the chaos, we lose our world.

Each movement speaks what words cannot,
In the depths, we are taught.
As we surrender to the night,
In the abyss, we find our light.

Through the labyrinth, we explore,
In every corner, there's so much more.
Together, we stretch beyond the thin,
In dances wild, our souls begin.

Imagination's Whisper

In quiet dreams, the shadows play,
Where thoughts take flight, they drift away.
A world unfolds in softest sighs,
With whispered truths beneath the skies.

Colors blend in twilight's fold,
Stories waiting to be told.
With every glance, the heart ignites,
A spark of wonder, pure delights.

In the depths of silent night,
Ideas blossom, take their flight.
A canvas painted with the soul,
Imagination makes us whole.

Gentle breezes bring the muse,
In softest hues, we find our cues.
For in the whispers, dreams align,
The universe begins to shine.

When hearts awaken, visions gleam,
Reality bends to a hopeful dream.
Embrace the magic, let it soar,
For in our minds, there's always more.

The Art of Vision

With every stroke, the canvas breathes,
A story woven through the leaves.
Brush dipped deep in colors bright,
Revealing dreams in morning light.

Eyes that see beyond the veil,
Charting paths where hearts can sail.
In every shadow, promise lies,
Transcending limits, soaring skies.

The rhythm flows like rivers wide,
Each splash of paint, a heartfelt guide.
Crafting worlds in vibrant scales,
Where imagination never fails.

From silence blooms a voice divine,
In art's embrace, our spirits shine.
Capturing moments, pure and true,
In every piece, a glimpse of you.

Be bold, create, let colors sing,
For in this art, we find our wings.
Express yourself, let visions blend,
In the heart of art, we transcend.

Colors of the Mind

Each hue unfolds a tale untold,
A spectrum rich, and bright, and bold.
In shades of fire, the passions glow,
While tranquil blues help sorrows flow.

Emerald greens of nature's grace,
Awake the spirit, set the pace.
Through vibrant colors, visions stir,
In every brush, the thoughts confer.

With golden yellows, warmth embraced,
Energizing every space.
A dance of colors, flowing free,
Reflecting depths of you and me.

The canvas whispers secrets deep,
In every layer, dreams we keep.
A kaleidoscope of heart and soul,
In this wide world, we find our whole.

Let every color tell its tale,
For in this art, we will not fail.
Embrace the hues, the shades divine,
In colors bright, our hearts entwine.

Muse on the Run

Chasing whispers on a winding path,
The muse escapes, igniting wrath.
With fleeting thoughts like morning dew,
I grasp for moments, fleeting, true.

Through wild fields, she dances free,
An ethereal spirit, can’t you see?
Her laughter echoes in the air,
In every heart, she plants a flare.

With open eyes, I seek her trace,
In shadows deep, I find her grace.
An artful spark, she lights the flame,
And in her chase, I find my name.

From twilight's dream to dawn’s bright glance,
The muse compels, she leads the dance.
In every heartbeat, she remains,
A wanderer in joy and pains.

So let me run, let spirit soar,
With muse beside, we’ll explore.
In every breath, in every sigh,
Together, we reach for the sky.

The Song of the Unseen

Whispers in the shadowed night,
A melody that's out of sight.
Fleeting echoes in the air,
Softly dancing, unaware.

Hidden truths, a gentle sigh,
Notes that drift and softly fly.
In the silence, secrets bloom,
Haunting rhythms fill the room.

Ethereal chords of forgotten dreams,
Flowing through like silver streams.
They linger long, yet come and go,
A symphony of ebb and flow.

In shadows deep, the heart can hear,
The whispered song, so crisp and clear.
An unseen world, it sings to me,
In every note, a hidden key.

So listen close, let silence lead,
To the songs of thought and deed.
For in the unseen, a truth is spun,
A melody for everyone.

Mosaics of Emotion

Fragments of color, burst and sway,
Each hue tells a tale today.
Joy resides in bright, warm light,
While sadness drapes in shadows tight.

Tears glisten like drops of rain,
Sorrow stitched with threads of pain.
Hope shines bright in vibrant tones,
In every heart, a place it owns.

Laughter dances on the breeze,
A vibrant note that brings us peace.
The mosaic shifts with each heartbeat,
A canvas where all colors meet.

Memories whisper through each shade,
In the tapestry we've made.
With every feeling, layers grow,
A masterpiece, an inner glow.

Celebrate the highs and lows,
In every moment, life bestows.
For in each piece, a story flows,
A mosaic, where true love shows.

The Language of Light

Sunrise paints the morning sky,
Golden rays that softly tie.
Every beam a word unspoken,
In the light, our hearts awaken.

Shadows stretch and light retreats,
In the twilight, beauty meets.
Colors blend in perfect harmony,
A symphony of light's decree.

Through the prism, visions dance,
Illuminating every chance.
Reflecting dreams that flicker bright,
In the glow, we find our sight.

Night's embrace brings stars to play,
Whispers of the end of day.
Moonlight bathes the world in grace,
A gentle touch, a soft embrace.

In every ray, a story told,
The language of light, pure and bold.
Through its warmth, our souls take flight,
In the silence, we find the light.

Beyond the Horizon

Where sky meets land, dreams take flight,
Colors clash in fiery light.
A place where the ocean kisses the day,
Beyond the horizon, we find our way.

Mountains rise, proud and tall,
Guardians of secrets, they whisper and call.
In the breeze, tales intertwine,
Of journeys taken, both yours and mine.

The sun dips low, the stars ignite,
A canvas painted with pure delight.
Each moment cherished, a treasure to keep,
Beyond the horizon, our hopes leap.

Adventure lies in every breath,
A dance between life and death.
As we chase the fading light,
Beyond the horizon, hearts take flight.

In the spaces where dreams align,
We find our truth, we find our sign.
Beyond the horizon, we seek to roam,
In every step, we build our home.

Serendipity's Sketch

A chance encounter shines bright,
Echoes of laughter in the night.
Moments caught in fleeting grace,
A dance of fate in time and space.

Unexpected paths we tread,
With every word, a story spread.
Brushstrokes of joy paint the sky,
In serendipity, we learn to fly.

Wander through the tangled maze,
Find beauty in the small, the haze.
Whispers of dreams in the air,
Each twist and turn leads us somewhere.

Captured hearts beneath the stars,
With open minds, we find who we are.
In shadows deep, light will break,
A canvas of life, our own to make.

Together we sketch this grand design,
A map of wonder, yours and mine.
Through serendipity, we weave our thread,
In every heartbeat, a life well led.

Labyrinth of the Imagination

A winding path of endless thought,
Where dreams are chased and battles fought.
Echoes linger in vibrant view,
Thoughts take flight, painted in hue.

Corners twist, and shadows play,
In the maze where mind holds sway.
Ideas dance on wisps of air,
Each turn reveals a vision rare.

Creativity’s door swings wide,
Inviting worlds to step inside.
In the labyrinth, we find our muse,
To wander freely, to learn, to choose.

Maps of wonder in the night,
Guided by an inner light.
In this realm, we soar and glide,
The heart and soul entwined, our guide.

Through every twist, we seek the truth,
Uncover wisdom, rekindle youth.
In the labyrinth, we are free,
Imagination's key unlocks the sea.

Gossamer Threads of Thought

Like whispers caught in morning dew,
Thoughts weave stories old and new.
Delicate strands of woven light,
Illuminate the depth of night.

Fragile dreams on silken breeze,
Carried softly through the trees.
In each thread, a vision glows,
Binding hearts where wisdom flows.

Connected by this fragile lace,
We find meaning in our place.
Each moment shared, a golden strand,
In the tapestry, we take our stand.

Gossamer paths lead us afar,
Guided by the inner star.
In the weaving, we create,
A network rich, where we relate.

With gentle hands, we pull the thread,
In every bond, sweet love is bred.
Together we spin this endless tale,
In gossamer dreams, our hearts set sail.

Fables in the Wind

Stories carried on the breeze,
Whispered secrets among the trees.
Tales of wonder, lost in time,
Echoes soft, in rhythm and rhyme.

Fables woven with ancient lore,
Open hearts to what’s in store.
Lessons learned from ages past,
In every word, a spell is cast.

Beneath the sky, the tales take flight,
In shadows cast by fading light.
Their whispers linger, soft and clear,
Fables in the wind, forever near.

Characters dance in twilight's glow,
Teaching truths that ebb and flow.
With every gust, a story spun,
In every breeze, we’re all as one.

Conversations held with the night,
Fables shared in gentle light.
In the magic of the wind we find,
The timeless bond of heart and mind.

From Sparks to Fire

In the twilight's gentle glow,
Sparks of passion dance and soar,
Whispers of dreams ignite the night,
Fueling flames forevermore.

With every flicker, stories grow,
Embers sing in heart's delight,
Words alight like shooting stars,
Guiding souls through endless flight.

Moments flash like lightning bright,
Kindling hearts that dare aspire,
Through the shadows, they will shine,
Transforming darkness into fire.

Friends gather close, the warmth embraced,
United by this vibrant blaze,
Hand in hand, we chase the sparks,
Crafting memories that amaze.

As the night begins to fade,
Fires dim but never die,
In our hearts, the flames remain,
From sparks, we reach beyond the sky.

The Whispering Muse

Softly she speaks, the muse divine,
Woven dreams in twilight's seam,
Her voice like silk, a gentle chime,
Guiding thoughts where shadows gleam.

With every brush, colors arise,
Painting worlds both bright and fair,
In her gaze, a universe,
Crafted from our hidden care.

In whispered words, she brings to life,
The stories linger, filled with grace,
In silent moments, inspiration,
Igniting creativity's embrace.

Dance through the realms, pure and wild,
Capture time with every line,
Through bitter trials, sweet and mild,
Her shadows fall like sacred wine.

Together we tell tales untold,
In her arms, the heart finds peace,
With every verse, the magic's bold,
In whispers, all our fears release.

Notes from a Wandering Dream

In the stillness where echoes play,
A journey starts on paths unseen,
Through realms where night and day,
Entwine in hues of softest sheen.

With every step, a note is penned,
A melody of thoughts unfurled,
From whispers carried on the breeze,
A soundtrack for this dreaming world.

Each soul I meet, a fleeting line,
A story wrapped in whispered fate,
Like stars that shine, then fade away,
We weave our songs before too late.

As clouds drift by in endless skies,
Each note a sigh, a breath, a dream,
In wandering, we find our ties,
Unraveled thoughts, a silken seam.

When morning breaks, the echoes fade,
But memories linger, soft and bright,
With every dream, new paths are laid,
In notes that stir the heart to flight.

Kaleidoscopic Visions

Swirling colors, bright and bold,
A canvas born of endless light,
Fragments dance, stories unfold,
In mosaic dreams, we take flight.

Patterns twisting, shapes collide,
In the chaos, beauty found,
Each moment's spark, a vibrant guide,
Painting worlds in hues profound.

Reflections play in shifting space,
An artist's heart, a prism's song,
Every glance, a new embrace,
A journey where the lost belong.

Through crystal visions, life ignites,
Creating wonders with each turn,
In kaleidoscopes of starry nights,
We seek the passions that we yearn.

As worlds collide in swirling dreams,
We hold the magic in our hands,
In every color, hope redeems,
And love, the thread that understands.

Uncharted Paths of Thought

In silence deep, the mind takes flight,
Through winding trails, in search of light.
Each twist and turn, a question posed,
New realms of wisdom, yet undisclosed.

With every step, a whisper calls,
To venture forth where mystery sprawls.
Unraveled visions dance in dreams,
A tapestry woven from silent streams.

In shadows cast, the truth is hid,
Untamed roads where few have bid.
The heart leads on, through woods unknown,
On paths where seeds of thought are sown.

A compass found in fleeting time,
Charting courses without a rhyme.
Embrace the journey, heed the call,
For in uncharted lands, we learn to fall.

And should we stumble, rise anew,
From every doubt, a spark breaks through.
For thoughts once lost, in depths of night,
Grow wings in dawn's resplendent light.

The Canvas of Dreams

Upon a canvas, colors blend,
With every stroke, our hearts extend.
Imagined scenes, bold and bright,
Where shadows play with beams of light.

Visions twirl in painter's hands,
A symphony of bright demands.
Each hue a whisper, soft and clear,
In every corner, dreams draw near.

The palette speaks of hopes untold,
A story waiting to unfold.
With gentle brush, we paint the skies,
In vibrant shades, our spirits rise.

From deep cerulean to fiery red,
The essence captured, words unsaid.
In every layer, life reflected,
A masterpiece, time’s hand directed.

As twilight puts her coat of gray,
The canvas glows, the dreams will stay.
With every heartbeat, art will gleam,
In this bright realm, we dare to dream.

Echoes of Inspiration

In the quiet, echoes hum,
Whispers of where our thoughts come from.
They ripple through the open air,
Inviting us to dream and dare.

From mountains high to valleys low,
In every heart, the embers glow.
A symphony of voices sing,
In every pause, the heart will spring.

The past resounds, the future calls,
In all of us, the spirit stalls.
Yet in the silence, we can find,
The threads that weave the ties that bind.

Listen closely, let it soar,
These echoes hold the ancient lore.
They guide our steps, ignite the spark,
In shadows deep, they leave their mark.

With every echo, inspiration flows,
In dreams it nurtures, hope it sows.
So let the whispers take their flight,
Together we'll emerge in light.

The Alchemy of Ideas

In the cauldron of thought, we stir our dreams,
Combining whispers, hopes, and schemes.
A pinch of courage, a dash of grace,
Transforming shadows, we find our place.

Ideas spark in the darkest night,
Leading us forth with vibrant light.
From simple thoughts, a world can grow,
Fulfilling visions, helping us know.

With every thought, a potion brews,
Imagination flows, with endless hues.
We mold the future with hands unseen,
In the alchemy of what might have been.

The catalysts of change, we call our own,
In the furnace of passion, our seeds are sown.
A blend of wisdom, wild and free,
In this grand alchemy, we dare to be.

So raise a glass, toast the unknown,
For in our hearts, the fire has grown.
To forge new paths, with thoughts aligned,
Creating magic, one thought combined.

Mindscapes Unbound

In realms where thoughts collide,
Ideas soar and glide.
Colors swirl in endless flight,
Shaping visions, day and night.

A whisper calls from deep inside,
Awakening dreams that hide.
The mind a labyrinth, vast and wide,
Exploring paths where hearts confide.

With echoes soft of hopes untold,
Stories in the mind unfold.
In silence, secrets start to bloom,
Creating worlds within the room.

Fragments woven, threads of light,
Guiding us through endless night.
Each thought a spark, each wish a flame,
In this dance, we find our name.

Unbound, released from ground and fear,
In dreams we see what's crystal clear.
The canvas of the heart expands,
As longing slips through tender hands.

The Canvas of Dreams

A brushstroke vibrant, rich and bold,
In whispered hues, the tales are told.
Each splash of color, each line defined,
Crafts the visions of the mind.

In twilight’s grace, a world takes form,
A harmony, both soft and warm.
From shadows deep, to brightened skies,
A masterpiece that never lies.

Imagination paints the air,
With visions floating everywhere.
As feelings tumble, brightly gleam,
Together we create our dream.

Each layer adds its own sweet song,
In this expanse where we belong.
A canvas stretched across the night,
Hold tight to dreams, let hearts take flight.

With every stroke, a spark ignites,
Revealing paths and endless sights.
The beauty flows, our spirits soar,
On the canvas, we explore.

A Dance of Shadows

In twilight’s embrace, shadows play,
As whispers blend with fading day.
Figures twist in gentle sway,
A dance of night, a soft ballet.

The silence hums a haunting tune,
Beneath the watchful, watchful moon.
Patterns shift, then intertwine,
In the depths where dreams align.

With every step, the echoes grow,
A tale untold begins to flow.
In flickers soft, the heartbeats race,
In shadows' waltz, we find our place.

Through veils of night, the stories weave,
In every turn, we learn to believe.
The light retreats, the darkness sings,
In this dance, our spirit springs.

So let the shadows guide our way,
In rhythms that the heart won’t sway.
In unity, both bold and bright,
We surrender to the night.

The Muse's Tapestry

Threads of thought in colors blend,
Each moment stitched is never spent.
A tapestry where dreams entwine,
In patterns formed, our souls align.

With gentle hands, the weaver twirls,
Creating magic, banners unfurl.
Each knot a wish, each stitch a tear,
In joy and sorrow, we find care.

The whispers dance through fabric fine,
In every shade, a spark divine.
Truths unfold in tranquil seams,
As life reveals its hidden themes.

With every thread, a story spun,
Lives connect, two hearts as one.
In rich embrace, the colors glow,
Through this masterpiece, our hearts flow.

The muse inspires with every hue,
In every heartbeat, fresh and new.
A tapestry of love and light,
In each design, a shared delight.

The Spark Within

In shadows deep, a fire glows,
Igniting dreams only the heart knows.
Whispers breathe life into the still,
A flicker of hope, a dance of will.

Beneath the surface, a pulse beats strong,
Echoing loud, a powerful song.
The essence of life, a radiant spark,
Guiding the lost through paths of dark.

With every breath, a chance reborn,
From ashes of doubt, like a new dawn.
Embrace the light, let courage soar,
In the heart of chaos, there's so much more.

Awaken the soul, let passion ignite,
Chase after dreams that shimmer bright.
For in the depths of the quiet night,
The spark within, a guiding light.

Threads of Possibility

In woven strands, our hopes entwine,
Each choice a stitch, a sacred sign.
Between the moments, futures spread,
A tapestry where dreams are fed.

Colors burst with every breath,
Weaving stories, defying death.
With hands outstretched, we mold the clay,
Crafting paths in our own way.

The loom of time, it weaves so fine,
Patterns emerge, we start to align.
In the chaos, find your thread,
A journey awaits, where fear has fled.

Dreamers gather, a vibrant blend,
In threads of chance, our hearts transcend.
Together we rise, embracing the flow,
In this rich fabric, our spirits grow.

Celestial Blueprints

Stars align in infinite space,
Drawing maps of cosmic grace.
Guiding souls through twilight's seam,
In the vastness, we find our dream.

Constellations whisper secrets bright,
In shadows deep, they bring us light.
Every twinkle, a story told,
Of journeys brave and hearts of gold.

In the cosmic dance, we find our place,
Navigating through time and grace.
With every heartbeat, a spark ignites,
In celestial blueprints, our fate unites.

Map of the heavens, a sacred scroll,
Tracing the lineage of the soul.
Under the night, our spirits roam,
In celestial blueprints, we are home.

Celestial Choreography

The moonlit stage, where shadows play,
Stars like dancers in grand ballet.
Across the night, a cosmic flow,
In celestial choreography, we glow.

Planets glide with grace so rare,
A symphony of silence fills the air.
Each movement speaks of love and chance,
In the ether, we find our dance.

The universe hums a gentle tune,
Guiding us under the watchful moon.
In every twirl, a heartbeat shared,
A cosmic embrace, perfectly paired.

With every step, a story unfolds,
In stardust dreams, our fate beholds.
Join the dance, let your spirit soar,
In celestial choreography, forever more.

Mysteries in Motion

Whispers dance on the breeze,
Secrets hidden in the trees.
Footsteps echo through the night,
Shadows shimmering, soft and light.

Moments fleeting like a dream,
Life unfolds in silent stream.
Patterns weave and then unwind,
In every glance, a truth to find.

Time's embrace, a gentle guide,
Through the realms where thoughts collide.
Visions blur, then come alive,
In this place where dreams can thrive.

Journey forth, let spirits soar,
Unlock the mysteries at the core.
With each heartbeat, sense the grace,
Of fleeting time in sacred space.

Eyes wide open to the stars,
Mapping journeys near and far.
In the motion, life unfolds,
Mysteries waiting to be told.

Garden of Ideas

In the silence, seeds take root,
Thoughts like blossoms, fresh and cute.
Cultivated with patient care,
Ideas bloom in fragrant air.

Sunshine kisses every bud,
Nurtured deep within the mud.
Colors burst, a vivid show,
In this garden, dreams can grow.

Winds of change bring new designs,
Crafting paths in twisting vines.
Every whisper, gently sown,
In this patch, a world unknown.

Harvest joy, and share the yield,
In this space where hearts are healed.
Imagination's gentle hand,
Plants the seeds across the land.

Breathe the essence, taste the air,
In this garden, free of care.
Each thought sprouted, bright and clear,
A sanctuary always near.

Fragments of Inspiration

Scattered moments like a breeze,
Whirling thoughts that aim to please.
Picking pieces from the sky,
Shimmering sparks that catch the eye.

Silent whispers, echoes loud,
Filling hearts, a vibrant crowd.
Fragments gather, stories blend,
Inspiration, a faithful friend.

Chasing shadows, chasing light,
Finding beauty in the night.
Each a puzzle, each a rhyme,
Crafted gently, touched by time.

Hopes and dreams, a scattered trail,
Leading forth, we must not fail.
In every piece, a glimpse we see,
Of the whole, a symphony.

Gather close, as lanterns glow,
In the dark, our spirits flow.
Fragments join to form the song,
A melody where we belong.

The Light Beyond Boundaries

Horizons stretching out of sight,
Chasing dawn, embracing light.
Walls that fade into the past,
In this realm, fears cannot last.

Up above, a canvas wide,
Colors blend on nature's side.
From shadows rise, a new embrace,
Finding strength in every space.

Voices echo, soft and clear,
Breaking barriers, drawing near.
Heartbeats sync in radiant glow,
In the light, we learn to grow.

Dreamers gather, hand in hand,
Together strong, we take a stand.
Leaving doubts along the way,
In this journey, night turns day.

From mountains high to oceans wide,
In this light, we turn the tide.
Boundaries fade, horizons call,
In the light, we conquer all.

Reveries Unchained

In twilight's glow, dreams lightly soar,
Whispers of hope forevermore.
Stars illuminate the silent night,
Guiding the heart towards the light.

Memories twirl in gentle grace,
Each thought a fragment of a trace.
Within the mind, a tapestry,
Woven threads of mystery.

Across the skies, the visions play,
Dancing on clouds, they drift away.
In every hue, a story spins,
Echoes of laughter, sorrow thins.

Awake to dreams that softly speak,
In every corner, secrets peek.
Unfurling tales of joy and pain,
In reveries, we break the chain.

With every dawn, the visions fade,
Yet in the heart, their essence stayed.
So let your dreams take flight and roam,
For in their grasp, we find our home.

The Dance of Innovation

In shadows deep, ideas ignite,
Sparks of change, a powerful sight.
With every twist, a new embrace,
Invention breathes in time and space.

Minds collide, like thunder's roar,
Concepts leap to open doors.
In harmony, they find their way,
Creating pathways, bright as day.

Crafted visions take their form,
Breaking limits, challenging norm.
A waltz of progress, bold and bright,
In every step, we chase the light.

From whispered dreams, foundations rise,
Innovation sings beneath the skies.
With every heartbeat, futures call,
Together we shall rise, not fall.

So let us dance through trials and fears,
In the rhythm of the years.
For in this waltz of endless chance,
We find our strength, we find our stance.

Whirlwind of Colors

A canvas breathes, alive and bold,
Filled with stories yet untold.
Brush strokes swirl, like winds in flight,
Every hue, a spark of light.

The crimson spills, the azure flows,
In vibrant tides, the vision grows.
Gold embraces, silver weaves,
Artistry glimmers in what it leaves.

Each color whispers, secrets shared,
In playful patterns, beauty's bared.
Through every shade, a tale is spun,
In this tempest, we are one.

Frames of life, both bright and gray,
Emotions dance, then slip away.
Yet in this whirlwind, we find grace,
In every fleeting, sacred space.

So paint your dreams with vibrant flair,
In every moment, let them bear.
A whirlwind of colors, wild and free,
Reflecting the soul’s deep tapestry.

Resonance of the Soul's Brush

With gentle strokes, the heart expresses,
Each color sings, while silence blesses.
A paintbrush dipped in vibrant fate,
Crafting the world we recreate.

In every swirl, a passion glows,
A dance of light that ebbs and flows.
The canvas pulses with a breath,
Defying time, embracing depth.

In whispers soft, the shades collide,
With every hue, the soul’s pride.
From darkness deep to radiant sun,
Each line drawn, a journey begun.

A palette rich with joy and strife,
Each stroke reflects the dance of life.
Between the strokes, a truth resides,
An echo of what the heart decides.

So let your spirit find its way,
With every brush, let colors play.
For in this art, the soul’s embraced,
In resonant whispers, life is traced.

Chronicle of the Unfamiliar

In whispers of night, shadows speak,
Where secrets retreat, and silence is bleak.
Paths untrodden wait, yearning for grace,
In the heart of the wild, time leaves no trace.

Wonders unfold in each timid glance,
As we dance with the winds, join the chance.
The stories of stars, they twinkle and weave,
An epic of hope, if you just believe.

On the edge of the world, dreams take flight,
With wings made of stardust, ready for night.
Each heartbeat a promise, to soar and to roam,
Fate intertwines, making the un-familiar our home.

In shadows and light, we find our way,
Through echoes of laughter, back to the day.
The chapters are written in hues of the soul,
An odyssey endless, forever whole.

So heed the call of the unknown afar,
For the path may be winding but leads to the star.
In the chronicle vast, we fashion our fate,
Boundless explorers, never too late.

Paintbrushes of Possibility

With colors unseen, we start to create,
A canvas of dreams, wide with fate.
Each stroke a whisper, each hue a sigh,
In the gallery of hope where visions fly.

The palette of life, rich and diverse,
Exploring the realms we so often traverse.
With every new shade, our spirits alight,
Painting the dawn, embracing the night.

Brushes of courage, dipped in the bold,
Crafting the stories that yearn to be told.
We splatter our fears, let the colors run free,
Revealing the beauty of what we could be.

In moments of silence, imagination swells,
Each canvas alive with the magic it tells.
With laughter and joy, we will dance and sing,
For every day holds a new offering.

So take up your brush, weave your delight,
In the tapestry woven of dreams shining bright.
With paintbrushes of possibilities wide,
Create your own story, let your heart guide.

The Labyrinth of Fantasy

In dreams enshrined, the labyrinths call,
Winding and turning, through shadows we crawl.
Each corner reveals a wonder untamed,
In the heart of the maze, our spirits are framed.

With echoes of magic that lead us astray,
We navigate mysteries that dance in the grey.
A flicker of light shows the path to pursue,
As we wander together, our fantasies grew.

A tapestry woven of whispers and light,
Every twist of the turning brings forth delight.
In this realm of the bold, we surrender our fears,
Embracing the laughter, the joy, and the tears.

Beneath the starlit sky, the secrets align,
Each story a thread, endlessly entwined.
In the labyrinth vast, we find our own way,
With hearts ever open, we dance through the day.

In the garden of dreams where shadows retreat,
Magic unfurls at each nameless street.
The labyrinth beckons, a journey divine,
Where each twist and turn, our souls intertwine.

Seeding New Realities

In gardens of thought, we plant our seeds,
Dreams take root, fulfilling our needs.
With waters of vision, we nurture the ground,
Where hopes bloom bright, and possibilities surround.

Each sprout a whisper of what we can be,
Reaching for sunlight, breaking free.
In the soil of intention, we patiently wait,
To harvest the future, in love we create.

Branches extend, reach for the sky,
As the winds carry wishes on dreams flying high.
In fields of potential, the seasons will change,
But the roots of our hopes will always remain.

Through storms and through trials, we carry the flame,
In the heart of our souls, we cherish the same.
Seeding the world with moments of grace,
New realities flourish, time finds its place.

So plant every dream, let your spirit grow,
In the lushness of life, let your essence flow.
For every small seed can alter the fate,
In the tapestry woven, love's never too late.

Explorations in Color

In every hue, a story flows,
Brush strokes dance where no one goes.
Crimson dreams and azure skies,
Nature's canvas, bold and wise.

Emerald forests whisper low,
Golden sunsets put on a show.
Each color sings of worlds unseen,
Adventure calls where hearts have been.

A palette rich with tales untold,
In violet shades, the brave and bold.
Paint the life you wish to see,
In every shade, set your heart free.

Through brush and dream, we wander far,
Guided by the north star's spar.
Let colors merge, let spirits soar,
In every stroke, we find much more.

The canvas waits, our hearts align,
In explorations, love will shine.
With every color, we take flight,
Creating beauty, day and night.

Enigmas of the Heart

A flutter there, a whispered breath,
Secrets dwell beyond life's depth.
Within the heart, a riddle hides,
Love's sweet chaos confides and guides.

Two souls entwined, a dance so rare,
In longing glances, we lay bare.
Desires wrapped in shadows' cloak,
Echoes of promises softly spoke.

The heart can break, yet fiercely heal,
Lessons learned with wounds that feel.
Hope's gentle muse will light the way,
In every dusk, we'll find the day.

Enigmas spin with threads of fate,
What was lost, we learn to create.
In every sigh, in every tear,
The heart finds ways to persevere.

So hold it close, this beating art,
Together we unlock the heart.
In shadows cast, our truths reveal,
In love's embrace, we learn to heal.

Wings of Wonder

With wings unfurled, we start to glide,
In realms of dreams, we seek to bide.
Clouds whisper soft, the winds ignite,
Adventures vast, in star-kissed night.

Feathers brush against the sky,
As boundless thoughts begin to fly.
In every soar, a tale unfolds,
Of hopes to chase and dreams to hold.

The horizon calls, a beckoning light,
With every beat, we chase the flight.
Through valleys deep and mountains tall,
In every journey, we rise and fall.

Let wonder guide with gentle grace,
In every corner, find a space.
To breathe the magic, feel the cheer,
With wings of wonder, have no fear.

So take the leap, embrace the dare,
With open hearts, we journey there.
Through skies of endless dreams anew,
In every moment, we are true.

The Ink of Revolution

With every pen, we write the change,
In ink, the world feels free and strange.
Ideas flow like rivers wide,
Unraveling truths that time can't hide.

Voices rise, a chorus bold,
In every phrase, our dreams unfold.
The ink, a sword; the words, a fight,
For justice sought, we spark the light.

Pages turn, the battles rage,
In every story, we turn the page.
The power to rise is in our hands,
With ink as glue, our restless bands.

A revolution written clear,
Through every stanza, face the fear.
In solidarity, we stand tall,
In the ink of revolution, we hear the call.

So let the lines empower the soul,
In every verse, we find our role.
For words can spark the fire anew,
With ink and dreams, we'll see it through.

The Hidden Architect

In shadows deep, plans intertwine,
Blueprints of dreams in a world divine.
Hands craft the silence, whispers of fate,
Brick by brick, they open the gate.

A canvas unseen, yet colors abound,
Where thoughts and ideas dance all around.
Sculpting the essence with every breath,
Life is the art that transcends death.

Structures emerge from the quiet gloom,
Built on the echoes that spark and bloom.
Foundations of passion, strong and true,
The architect's vision breaks through the blue.

Hidden in plain sight, the magic flows,
Creating a haven where wonder grows.
Each line, each curve, a story to tell,
The architect weaves in a lyrical spell.

In the hushed evening, the plans take flight,
An unseen glory, a dance of light.
With dreams as their guide, they boldly chart,
The hidden architect breathes life to art.

Vortex of Visions

Spin of the cosmos, where dreams collide,
A whirling dance in time's endless tide.
Ideas converge in radiant hues,
In the vortex of visions, all worlds fuse.

Swirling whispers call from afar,
Echoes of stardust, a guiding star.
They paint the abyss with colors so bright,
Illuminating pathways lost in the night.

Time bends and stretches, the future unclear,
Yet in this whirlwind, there's nothing to fear.
Capture the moments that swirl and blend,
In the heart of the vortex, reality bends.

Through layers of thought, beyond the mundane,
Fleeting glimpses of joy and pain.
In this astral dance, the truth finds a way,
Launching our spirits, come what may.

Ride the tempest, let go, be free,
For in every vision lies possibility.
Lose not your wonder, embrace the spree,
In the vortex of visions, together we'll be.

Dreamcatchers of Thought

Threads of the mind, woven with care,
Catching the dreams that float in the air.
In the silence, they whisper and weave,
A tapestry rich, for those who believe.

Fleeting glimpses of hopes on the breeze,
Dancing through shadows like leaves on the trees.
Each strand a story, hidden yet bright,
In the dreamcatchers' web, they shimmer with light.

We set our intentions with love and with grace,
Entwined they linger, in time they embrace.
Hold close these wishes, let no one take flight,
For dreams are the fabric that colors the night.

With every heartbeat, a vision can bloom,
Awakening whispers from silence and gloom.
In the realm of the heart, let your spirit roam,
For dreamcatchers guide us, remind us of home.

So let your thoughts soar, unguarded and free,
Capture the magic, let it be.
In the web of creation, together we'll find,
The endless potential of heart and of mind.

The Pulse of the Unseen

In the quiet spaces, the heartbeat rings,
Where silence sings of forgotten things.
Echoes of life pulse through the dark,
Telling the tales that ignite a spark.

Beneath the surface, energy flows,
A rhythm that whispers; true magic grows.
The unseen forces, they guide our way,
With every heartbeat, dreams start to play.

Time moves like water, both gentle and fierce,
The pulse of existence, it bends, it pierces.
In the hidden moments, we come alive,
Learning to feel and daring to strive.

Listen closely, let your heart lead,
For in the unseen, we plant the seed.
With courage and kindness, we forge ahead,
The pulse of the unseen ignites the thread.

In the journey of life, we find our grace,
Moving with rhythm, we embrace our place.
For through the silence, a truth we glean,
The pulse of the unseen forever will be.

A Palette of Traces

Colors blend in soft embrace,
Memories swirl in a vibrant space.
Every brushstroke tells a tale,
Of fleeting moments, delicate and pale.

In shadows dance the hues so bright,
Carrying whispers of day and night.
A canvas holds the heart's refrain,
In silence speaks the joy and pain.

Life's fleeting strokes, a wondrous art,
Echoes linger, never depart.
Through every shade, stories unfold,
In a spectrum of wander, brave and bold.

Touch of the sun, and kiss of the rain,
Nature's palette eases the strain.
With every color, emotions unfurl,
Painting the dreams of a dancing world.

So let the brush dance, let it glide,
Across the canvas, where secrets hide.
In every color, find your trace,
In this grand art, find your place.

The Flow of Thought

Ripples form in the mind’s stream,
Ideas flutter, a vibrant dream.
Words like water, they twist and flow,
Carving valleys where wonders grow.

In stillness, thoughts begin to race,
Chasing shadows, a fleeting chase.
Through storms of doubt and calm retreat,
The current brings truth, bittersweet.

Moments gather, like leaves that fall,
Whispers echo, the heart's call.
In quiet corners, sparks ignite,
Illuminating the velvet night.

Ideas born, like stars that shine,
In the vast universe of the mind.
Flowing freely, a river in flight,
Uncovering worlds, hidden from sight.

So catch the thoughts, let them surge,
With every breath, let ideas merge.
In this grand flow, let dreams alight,
Harness the magic, dance with the light.

Whispers of Imagination

In the quiet, dreams take flight,
Wings unfurl in the dark of night.
Voices call from realms afar,
Guiding souls like a distant star.

Colors paint the skies of mind,
In every shadow, wonders find.
Secrets murmur, softly they tease,
In the heart's forest, dancing trees.

Ethereal visions, a fleeting glance,
Each thought a note in a cosmic dance.
Through realms of magic, spirits roam,
In whispered tales, they find a home.

Laughter echoes, a song once sung,
Life’s tapestry, forever spun.
From silken threads of fleeting dreams,
Emerges truth, or so it seems.

So take a step beyond the known,
In whispered worlds, the seeds are sown.
Let imagination be your guide,
In every heartbeat, let dreams reside.

Dancing with the Muse

In twilight's glow, the muse arrives,
With whispered dreams and vibrant jives.
A waltz of thoughts, both soft and bold,
In every movement, stories unfold.

Through shadows cast by candlelight,
Creativity begins its flight.
With every twirl, inspiration blooms,
Filling the silence with fragrant tunes.

Holding hands with echoes past,
Moments linger, shadows cast.
The dance reveals the heart's embrace,
A sacred rhythm, a sacred space.

In playful steps, the soul takes lead,
Finding joy in every need.
With laughter bright and tears that rise,
In this grand dance, our spirits fly.

So let the muse take center stage,
In this dance, turn every page.
With open hearts, we shall not lose,
The magic found in dancing with the muse.

In the Eye of the Artist

In the stillness, colors blend,
A canvas waits, the touch of hand.
Each stroke a whisper, stories pour,
Visions captured, forever stored.

A flash of light, a shadow’s dance,
Life and dreams in a fleeting glance.
In every hue, a heartbeat shines,
Through art, the soul's voice intertwines.

With each creation, worlds unfold,
A tale of passion, silently told.
Brush and palette, a sacred trust,
In vibrant chaos, beauty's rust.

Frames that hold, yet set us free,
In every piece, a memory.
Infinite realms, yet one confined,
In the eye of the artist, love refined.

So let the colors freely play,
In the light of each dawning day.
For in each vision, we must find,
The echoes of a heart aligned.

Forgotten Realms of Imagination

In forgotten realms where shadows roam,
Ideas linger, seeking a home.
Winds of wonder softly sigh,
As dreams take flight and spirits cry.

Through twisted paths of time and space,
Lost are the voices, yet find their place.
A tapestry woven with threads of light,
Awakens the magic hidden from sight.

In ancient woods, where silence reigns,
Whispers of elves in gentle strains.
Mountains rise like giants bold,
Guarding treasures untold and old.

Floating castles in the sky,
Stars as lanterns, watch us fly.
In realms of wonder, let us stray,
Where hearts and dreams forever play.

So venture forth, let none confine,
The power of thoughts entwined.
For in this magic, we shall dwell,
In the whispers of stories we tell.

The Dreamer's Ark

In the stillness of the night,
Dreamers gather, spirits bright.
An ark of thoughts, a vessel grand,
Sailing forth to imagination’s land.

With sails of hope and stars as guide,
In the heart of dreams, we confide.
Waves of wonder carry us near,
To shores unknown, with no fear.

Through tempests wild and tranquil waters,
Where every dreamer is a daughter or son.
Each story woven, each vision cast,
The echoes of future, shadows of past.

In the harbor of the mind’s delight,
We anchor dreams through the endless night.
For in this ark, our hopes set free,
To dance with eternity's melody.

So raise the sails, let currents flow,
In the dreamer's ark, the heart will glow.
Across the stars, we journey far,
Together guided by a wishful star.

Threads of Enchantment

In the loom of twilight, spells are spun,
Threads of magic in the setting sun.
With every twirl, a story weaves,
In the fabric of dreams, the heart believes.

Colors dancing, shimmering bright,
Tales whispered in the hush of night.
With a gentle hand and patient care,
Enchantment whispers, filling the air.

From golden fields to silver streams,
A tapestry woven of vibrant dreams.
Each thread a wish, a hope, a sigh,
Intertwined beneath the vast sky.

So let us gather, all hearts entwined,
With threads of joy, the lost shall find.
In this web of wonder, we unite,
In threads of enchantment, pure delight.

For in the art of weaving time,
We write our stories, sweetly sublime.
Through every knot, through every seam,
The threads of magic bind us in dreams.

Unfolding the Unseen

Behind the veil, shadows creep,
Mysteries in silence sleep.
Threads of time begins to weave,
A hidden world, we believe.

In soft whispers, secrets call,
Echoes dance within the hall.
Gentle hints, the heart can see,
Unseen paths await the free.

With each breath, new visions rise,
Awakening in quiet skies.
Through the fog, truths will stream,
Reality shifts like a dream.

In the stillness, dawn will break,
An open heart begins to wake.
To learn the art of being wise,
And deciphering hidden ties.

Let the journey lead the way,
Into realms where shadows play.
For in the dark, light will gleam,
As we uncover what we dream.

Colors of Curiosity

Brush of wonder paints the sky,
With each thought, our spirits fly.
Shades of joy, hues of delight,
In the quest, we find our light.

Each question stirs a vibrant hue,
Filling worlds with visions new.
In every answer, spark ignites,
A canvas rich with endless sights.

As we wander, colors blend,
Mysteries twist and never end.
From shades of doubt to brush of cheer,
The palette grows, bright and clear.

In shadows, hints of colors glow,
Mapping paths we yearn to know.
Curiosity, our guiding flame,
With every step, we play the game.

Through the prism, visions soar,
Unlocking dreams, forever more.
In the mosaic of our quest,
We find our truth and feel it best.

The Spark of Invention

In the stillness, ideas spark,
Flickering flames in the dark.
Thoughts collide and form anew,
A dance of minds, a world to view.

From whispers born, bold concepts rise,
Innovations wear no disguise.
With daring hearts, we take our stand,
To create the future, hand in hand.

In each failure, lessons hide,
A journey marked by hope and pride.
The chords of genius intertwine,
As visions shift, so do the lines.

A flicker turns to roaring flame,
Invention thrives, it knows no shame.
With every dream that breaks the mold,
We carve our tales, both brave and bold.

The spark ignites, it spreads so wide,
With passion as our guiding tide.
Together we will rise and dare,
To change the world, our thoughts laid bare.

Chasing Fragments of Genius

In the corners of our mind,
Glimmers of brilliance hard to find.
We chase the trails of fleeting thought,
Hoping for the gems we sought.

Through the maze, our heartbeats race,
In every shadow, we find a trace.
Fragments whisper, soft yet loud,
Manifesting dreams, strong and proud.

With open eyes, we dare to seek,
In the silence, genius speaks.
Ideas twirl, on wings they soar,
In the chase, we learn to explore.

As sparks ignite, we weave our fate,
In moments brief, we contemplate.
Each fragment holds a story's key,
Unlocking paths to set us free.

In the blur, our spirits blend,
With every twist, the journey bends.
To chase the light, to dare to dream,
In fragments found, we find our theme.

The Language of Innovation

Words like sparks ignite the night,
Ideas dance in shared delight.
Crafting visions, bold and bright,
In silence, we seek the light.

Each thought a thread in the loom,
Woven dreams, dispelling gloom.
Connections form, like flowers bloom,
Inspiring change, we find our room.

Voices rise, a chorus strong,
Breaking barriers, righting wrong.
With every step, we prove we belong,
In innovation, we grow lifelong.

Fear dissolves in the passion's fire,
Chasing visions we desire.
Every heartbeat adds to the choir,
Together, we climb ever higher.

In this realm where ideas flow,
The seeds of greatness, we sow.
Boundless paths, a vibrant glow,
In the language of change, we grow.

Embracing the Unconventional

In a world the norm defines,
We dance beyond the tangled lines.
With colors bright, our spirit shines,
Unleashing dreams, where freedom twines.

Straying paths, the heart's delight,
Finding beauty in the night.
With every leap, we take flight,
Embracing wonder, bold and bright.

Whispers echo, soft yet clear,
In the strange, we hold what's dear.
Unfurling wings, we conquer fear,
In the unconventional, we steer.

Curiosity, our guiding star,
Charting journeys, near and far.
Each different step, a work of art,
In disarray, we find our part.

Breaking chains, the heart beats free,
In the unknown, we find the key.
Together, with joyful glee,
We write the tale of you and me.

Melodies of the Unimaginable

In whispers soft, the music plays,
Notes that linger, a timeless haze.
From dreams unfurling, the spirit sways,
Tales of wonder weaves through days.

Rhythms rise from depths of night,
Releasing echoes, pure delight.
Each fleeting glance, a spark so bright,
In the heart, a beacon's light.

In silence found, the stories hum,
Filling spaces, a vibrant drum.
With every beat, a truth will come,
In the unimaginable, we succumb.

Voices blend in harmony's embrace,
Strange and lovely, a sacred space.
Together, we chase the haunting grace,
Of melodies lost in time's vast race.

Unseen worlds through sound unfold,
In every note, a tale retold.
For in each chord, we find the bold,
In the music, life’s secrets unfold.

The Pulse of Inspiration

Beneath the surface, a rhythm flows,
In every heartbeat, the spirit glows.
Each whispered thought a bridge that grows,
Inspiration's dance, the courage shows.

Bright horizons stretch and sway,
Chasing shadows, keeping gray at bay.
With every breath, we seize the day,
In every challenge, find the way.

Moments spark like fireworks bright,
Illuminating paths from night.
In the chaos, we find the light,
Inspiration guides with gentle might.

A symphony of hopes and fears,
As laughter flows, dissolving tears.
Weaving dreams through silent years,
In the pulse, our vision clears.

Together, we ride the vibrant tide,
In every tear, we find our pride.
For within this journey, side by side,
The pulse of life, our hearts collide.

Secrets of the Dreamweaver

In shadows deep, where whispers sigh,
A tapestry of dreams does lie.
With every thread, a tale unfolds,
Of secret worlds and treasures told.

Across the night, the visions flow,
The dance of thoughts, a gentle glow.
In silent nights, the heart shall weave,
The dreams we dare, the dreams believe.

Beneath the stars, we silently drift,
In realms where time and space do shift.
The Dreamweaver calls, her voice so sweet,
In every slumber, her magic meets.

A canvas vast, untouched by light,
Where fears dissolve and hopes take flight.
In whispered hues, our fears resign,
In dreams, we find what’s truly mine.

So close your eyes, embrace the night,
For in the dark, there's endless light.
The secrets whispered, softly spun,
In dreams, we rise, we are as one.

Flickers of Insight

In moments brief, the spark ignites,
A flicker bright in shadowed sights.
Wisdom dances in the haze,
Illuminating winding ways.

In stillness found, the mind unfolds,
In scattered thoughts, the truth beholds.
Each fleeting thought, like lightning's strike,
Reveals the path, the way we like.

Beneath the surface, the echoes rise,
A melody sung beneath calm skies.
Listen closely, let silence speak,
In quiet whispers, answers peek.

Through winding paths, the insights flow,
In every heart, the seeker's glow.
So chase the light, let wisdom sing,
Embrace the depth that knowing brings.

Each flicker shines, a guiding star,
In journeys near, and journeys far.
Stay awake, let visions guide,
In flickers bright, let dreams abide.

Orbiting Possibilities

In circles drawn, the stars align,
A dance of worlds, a grand design.
Each planet spins, a tale to share,
In cosmic space, we find our lair.

The moonlight casts a silver glow,
On paths untraveled, seeds we sow.
In every orbit, life's a chance,
A waltz of fate, a timeless dance.

Explorers bold, we chase the light,
With hearts aflame, we take our flight.
Infinite realms, horizons wide,
In every dream, new worlds reside.

From distant realms, the messages flow,
Each wave of thought, a chance to grow.
In orbit’s pull, we rise and fall,
In possibilities, we find our call.

So dare to dream, let visions soar,
In every turn, there's so much more.
Together we’ll roam the vast unknown,
Orbiting dreams, we’re never alone.

Navigator of the Mind's Eye

With compass drawn, the journey starts,
Through hidden realms, exploring hearts.
The map unfolds, each thought a guide,
In silent depths, our truths abide.

Navigating through the tangled maze,
With every choice, we weave the ways.
In shadows cast, the light will spark,
Illuminating paths in the dark.

Through valleys deep, and mountains high,
We seek the stars within the sky.
The heart a vessel, the mind the sail,
In every dream, we shall not fail.

Across the waves of thought we glide,
With every wave, we turn the tide.
A navigator with dreams in tow,
In the mind's eye, we learn and grow.

So chart your course, let courage rise,
In every journey, seek the prize.
For in the vastness of the soul,
The navigator finds their role.

A Tapestry of Thoughts

In the quiet of the night,
Dreams weave soft and light.
Threads of joy and sorrow,
We stitch together tomorrow.

Whispers catch the breeze,
Carried through the trees.
Each memory a hue,
Bringing life anew.

Colors blend and shift,
In this delicate gift.
A tapestry unfurls,
With the stories of the world.

Moments intertwine, bold,
Embrace the tales untold.
Every stitch a heartbeat,
Together, we feel complete.

In this woven design,
Thoughts and wishes align.
A canvas so profound,
In our hearts, love is found.

Waves of Whimsy

Dancing in the moonlight,
Stars sparkle, oh so bright.
With laughter that ignites,
Joy rides on the nights.

A breeze whispers tales,
Of ships and magical sails.
With whimsy as our guide,
We journey, hand in hand, side by side.

The ocean sings a song,
Where dreams and hopes belong.
In the rhythm, we sway,
Lost in the playful spray.

Shells scattered on the shore,
Each tells a story more.
With every wave that breaks,
A new adventure wakes.

Chasing after the tide,
Where secrets tend to hide.
In the depths, delight spins,
As the dance of life begins.

Beyond the Boundaries

Horizons stretch and bend,
Where the sky and land blend.
With courage, we will soar,
Free to explore much more.

The mountains call our name,
In the wild, we feel the flame.
Beyond the limits set,
Lies a world we won't forget.

Each step upon the trail,
Sparks a vision, all details.
Through valleys, we will weave,
In every moment, believe.

Stars guide us through the night,
Filling hearts with pure delight.
No fences hold our dreams,
We travel where joy streams.

In every twist and turn,
There's a new page to learn.
Beyond the boundaries drawn,
We find our way till dawn.

The Art of Serendipity

In life's gentle embrace,
We find our secret place.
Moments come and go,
In currents, we will flow.

Chance encounters unfold,
Stories waiting to be told.
With every turn we take,
We spark the dreams we make.

A smile shared by fate,
Opens wide the gate.
In the unexpected dance,
We find magic in a glance.

Through the twists and bends,
New beginnings, old friends.
With laughter echoing clear,
The art of joy draws near.

In life's serendipity,
We rediscover glee.
Every stumble leads the way,
To a brighter, brand new day.

Euphony of the Soul

In the whisper of the breeze,
Notes of joy begin to tease,
Melodies that softly sway,
Guiding hearts along the way.

Harmony in every breath,
Dancing lightly, conquering death,
With each beat our spirits rise,
Resonating with the skies.

Echoes of a distant dream,
Flowing like a gentle stream,
In this tune we find our light,
Casting shadows into night.

Rhythms woven, pure and clear,
Lifting souls, dissolving fear,
Every note a tender care,
Music sung within the air.

United by this sacred sound,
Lost in beauty, found profound,
In the euphony we share,
Lives entwined in perfect stare.

The Story Weaver

In twilight's hush, the tales begin,
Stitched with dreams, where thoughts have been,
Threads of gold and silver spun,
A legacy of all as one.

With every stitch, a memory glows,
Woven patterns, life bestows,
Narratives that dance and twine,
Binding past to future's line.

Characters with hearts ablaze,
Adventures, hope, and wondrous maze,
Each a voice in chorus bright,
Crafted by the weaver's light.

From fragile whispers to thunder's roar,
Every tale opens a door,
In the fabric of the day,
Stories guide us on our way.

The weaver's hand, a gentle touch,
Bringing forth the world, so much,
In every strand, a truth unfurls,
Connecting all our wondrous worlds.

Inspiration's Treasure Map

Beneath the stars, we seek the signs,
Paths like rivers, through the pines,
Ink on parchment, visions drawn,
Guiding hearts from dusk till dawn.

Every symbol, a spark ignites,
Whispers of our dreams in flights,
Marking treasures bold and bright,
Calling us to chase the light.

In the valleys, shadows play,
Carving routes to lead the way,
But courage fuels each fearless quest,
In the journey, we are blessed.

With every step, we carve the fate,
Together as we navigate,
Inspiration’s hand will guide,
In the map, our dreams abide.

As we follow, spirits soar,
Finding gold on distant shore,
In every secret that we find,
Treasures left by love, unconfined.

Sparks of the Sublime

In gentle glimmers, hope resides,
Cascading light, where beauty hides,
Each spark a moment, pure and rare,
Whispers of the universe's care.

Nature's breath, a vivid sigh,
Colors dancing, painting sky,
In every flicker, joy's embrace,
Soul's reflection, a sacred space.

Through twilight’s veil, the colors blend,
As day and night in harmony mend,
Sparks igniting, hearts awake,
In the silence, life’s a wake.

In each heartbeat, echoes play,
Infinite wonders on display,
Sublime moments shared so bright,
Guiding us toward the light.

Awakening, the spirit sings,
To every spark, the joy it brings,
In this dance of life, divine,
We find the love, the sacred line.

The Journey of the Unconventional

In paths untrod, we wander wide,
With courage as our only guide.
The map we forge, in silent dreams,
Where every step unveils new themes.

Through shadows deep, we weave our art,
Embracing each mishap and part.
With laughter loud, we break the mold,
Creating stories yet untold.

The world may frown, but we stand tall,
Through every rise, and every fall.
For in the strangeness lies our gain,
A tapestry of joy and pain.

With hearts unbound, we chase the light,
Finding beauty in the night.
The unconventional we wear proud,
A vibrant cloak, a colorful shroud.

Each twist and turn, a dance of fate,
Together we create, not wait.
In this grand journey, we ignite,
A spark of truth in endless night.

Resonance of the Unthought

In echoes faint, the whispers dwell,
Of thoughts unvoiced, their stories swell.
A realm where silence speaks so clear,
In shadows deep, we lose our fear.

The unsaid words, a tender bridge,
Connect our hearts, a fleeting ridge.
In stillness found, we start to dream,
Awakening nearness with a gleam.

In hidden realms, the feelings rise,
A tapestry of unseen ties.
The resonance within us grows,
A symphony that softly flows.

With every breath, the unthought sings,
Transforming lost into new wings.
A dance of souls, both far and near,
In harmony, we disappear.

In every heartbeat, magic brews,
The silent strength we can’t refuse.
We embrace what others have missed,
In unthought realms, we long exist.

The Altar of Inspiration

Upon this stage, where dreams awake,
We gather thoughts, our souls to stake.
In whispers soft, we light the flame,
To honor visions, none the same.

Each moment held, a precious gift,
Where minds converge, and spirits lift.
With open hearts, we dare to share,
Unfolding treasures, rare and fair.

In every glance, a spark ignites,
The altar glows with new delights.
Here creativity finds its voice,
Inviting every soul to rejoice.

Through paths of ink and colors bright,
We journey forth, embracing light.
For in this space, all dreams align,
The essence pure, the art divine.

With gratitude, we bow and pray,
To inspiration's gentle sway.
In this communion, hearts entwine,
A sacred bond, forever shine.

Wind Chimes of Aspiration

In gentle breezes, aspirations ring,
Each note a promise, sweetly sing.
The wind chimes dance, in sunlit grace,
Reflecting dreams in every space.

Soft melodies of hopes unfold,
A tapestry of brave and bold.
In every clang, a wish we cast,
The future bright, the shadows past.

With every gust, we reach up high,
To touch the dreams that fill the sky.
The whispers call with every sound,
In harmony, our spirits bound.

Together we rise, with hearts aligned,
In movement free, our paths combined.
In every chime, a tale we weave,
The echoes of what we believe.

So let the wind carry our song,
In unity, we all belong.
With open hearts, we chase the light,
In wind chimes true, our hopes take flight.

Sculpting Shadows

In twilight's grasp, shadows dance,
Figures formed in soft romance.
With hands of light, they take their shape,
Whispers echo, a dream escape.

Each curve and line, a story told,
In silver hues, the night is bold.
Casting spells with every sway,
Shadows weave where dreams will play.

Framing worlds in dark and light,
Artists crafting the veil of night.
Beneath the stars, they come alive,
In the darkness, we all thrive.

A canvas vast, the night unfolds,
Mysteries wrapped in silken folds.
Sculptors of the unseen realm,
In shadows, we find our helm.

So let us dance with shades so near,
In the silent whispers, we hear.
With every flicker, truths ignite,
Sculpting shadows, a pure delight.

The Fire Within

A flicker starts in soul's deep core,
A tiny flame, but yearns for more.
It crackles brightly, fierce and bold,
In its warmth, dreams are unrolled.

The heart ignites with vibrant hues,
Passions burn, and we can't refuse.
Through trials faced, it learns to soar,
In every struggle, it seeks to roar.

A blaze that lights the darkest night,
Within us all, it sparks the fight.
Nurture it, let it grow and thrive,
For in our fire, we're truly alive.

When winds of doubt begin to blow,
Feed the flame, let your courage show.
With every ember, we take our stand,
United, we rise, hand in hand.

So let it burn, let it brightly shine,
The fire within is yours and mine.
In unity, we find our way,
Together we ignite each day.

Blossoms of Originality

In gardens where wild colors bloom,
Original thoughts cast out the gloom.
Petals soft, in hues so rare,
Whispers of ideas float in air.

Each blossom tells a tale unique,
In vibrant strokes, they shyly peek.
From fertile minds, creativity flows,
In gentle winds, the wild flower grows.

Through seasons change, their beauty stays,
In every heart, a spark that plays.
A symphony of shapes and forms,
Against the norm, our spirit warms.

So let us plant in fields of dreams,
Watered with hope, or so it seems.
With every bud, a chance to thrive,
In originality, we come alive.

Together, let's nurture what we find,
In every flower, a piece of mind.
With love we tend, and joy we share,
Blossoms of originality everywhere.

The Laughter of Creation

In playful bursts, the cosmos sings,
Joyful notes on vibrant wings.
From chaos born, the order takes,
In laughter, life, the universe wakes.

Each moment shared, a spark of glee,
Creation dances, wild and free.
In every heartbeat, a rhythm flows,
Echoes of life, where magic grows.

With playful hands, the artist plays,
In every stroke, the spirit sways.
The laughter weaves through every thread,
Unraveling wonders, the heart is fed.

From shadows deep to skies so bright,
Creation's laughs take wondrous flight.
In joyous symphonies we find our way,
In laughter's arms, we long to stay.

So let us dance in creation's grace,
With smiles and wonder, we embrace.
For in each giggle, a spark divine,
The laughter of creation, forever shine.

Printed in the USA
CPSIA information can be obtained
at www.ICGtesting.com
LVHW020731190924
791513LV00003B/61

9 789916 877203